OSKAR KOKOSCHKA

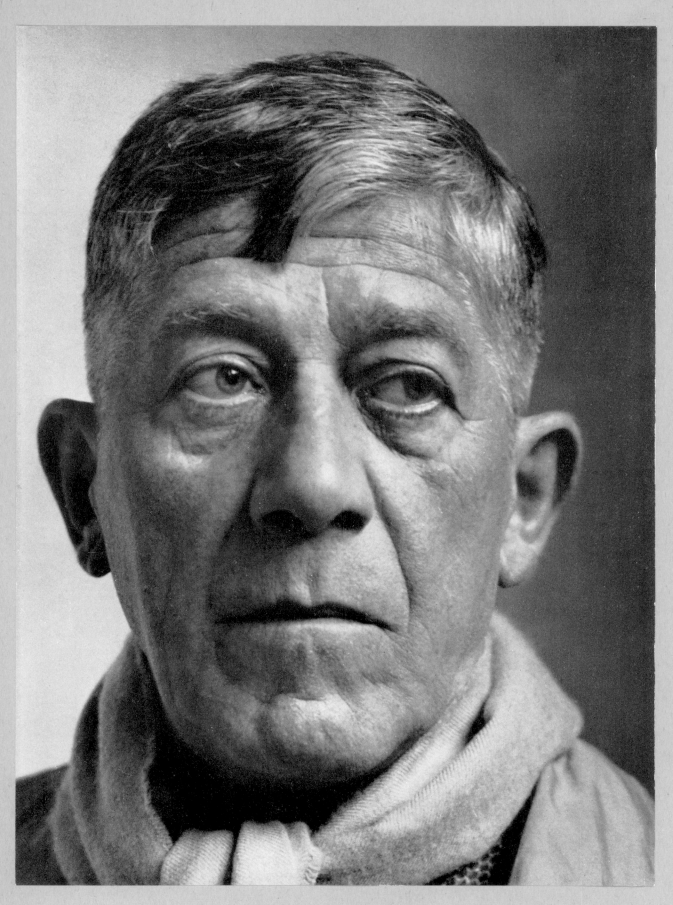

OSKAR

KOKOSCHKA

Text by Bernhard Bultmann

50 colour plates, 23 drawings and lithographs

THAMES AND HUDSON

TRANSLATED FROM THE GERMAN BY MICHAEL BULLOCK

CONTENTS

INTRODUCTION   *page* 7

KOKOSCHKA'S LIFE AND WORK   11

THE PLATES   43

BIBLIOGRAPHICAL NOTES   129

LIST OF ILLUSTRATIONS   131

The measurements of paintings are given in inches. Height precedes width.

In the captions to the colour plates the letters HMW followed by a number, refer to the comprehensive catalogue of Kokoschka's work prepared by Hans Maria Wingler

The magic of art is the only one that does not rest upon a superstition

OSKAR KOKOSCHKA

The significance of Oskar Kokoschka's work lies beyond aesthetic analysis or art-historical categories. It cannot be defined in such terms. Repeated attempts have been made to label it, to render it universally accessible and fit it into a general scheme of things by applying to it such descriptive titles as 'Expressionism', 'expressive Impressionism', 'modern revival of Danubian Baroque' and so forth. None of these designations is adequate, though there is some justification for all of them. Kokoschka's work is that of an individual who stands firmly within the mainstream of tradition, but who completely transforms what he takes over from this tradition, turning it into the instrument of an entirely personal and at times highly idiosyncratic record of his encounter with reality. Kokoschka's significance does not lie in his having found or invented a style, a secure vantage-point from which a given aesthetic reality is always accessible. His path as a painter is not steady and assured; it is a series of new departures, a perpetual readiness to expose himself to visual reality. This continuous readiness to expose himself means that Kokoschka's pictures are always painted under new conditions, in a new relationship to reality. They are not the outcome of a preconceived idea of the picture as such or of external reality, nor do they spring from the desire to pin down a transitory moment; each picture is a bridge between one moment and the next, an attempt to penetrate into the deeper reality below externals.

This may explain the inventive fertility and diversity of Kokoschka's work as a painter and also the difficulty of arriving at an adequate interpretation of it. It is difficult for the spectator to find his way about among these works, to do justice to each individual picture. Most of his admirers value their own particular version of Kokoschka, particular periods and particular pictures, remaining indifferent towards the rest. Kokoschka's work makes great demands upon the spectator. Again and again he throws away the chance of seducing the spectator with ready-made forms; again and again he demands that the spectator lay himself open to the new and unfamiliar, thereby offering him an aesthetic pleasure that is all the more acute because of its unfamiliarity.

By repeatedly adopting a new attitude to the scene around him and surrendering himself entirely to the momentary situation, however, Kokoschka actually succeeds in getting more into his pictures than the outward situation. His portraits show the 'inner face' of his subjects, combining past, present and future in one portrayal; his landscapes open up a vista through the typical, as embodied in the visual reality of the moment, to something eternal that lies beyond it, by this very fact isolating the truly specific element in this momentary reality. Kokoschka wishes to see more than the play of light on the surface and to create more than a painted surface. But he also wishes to do more than merely depict himself, more than merely create an expression of himself in a certain situation; he is trying to confront and find himself in his work. As a first step towards grasping the meaning of his work, let us therefore endeavour, not to place it in an art-historical category, but to see how art as he understands it is an ultimate aspect of our existence.

Art is important and fruitful when it transcends what is available to our senses, when it shows images alien to our experience, when it opens our eyes and makes us ask questions. The ancient Chinese distinguished between two types of painters. The first practised painting as a craft for the purpose of embellishing objects of everyday use, decorating walls, adding to man's enjoyment of life, and operating within the firmly established canon of aesthetic harmony. To the second, painting was given as an art, as a spiritual zone within which the painter could surrender himself in the fullest possible degree to the visible, in order to stand face to face with reality in the work of art, to destroy the outer crust, the façade, and to discern and portray the essence behind it, which is mysterious, flowing, eternal, alive and beyond the reach of conceptual thought. In Buddhist and Confucian China painters of this kind were called 'monk-painters', because they had to dedicate themselves and their lives entirely to this task of perceiving and making visible. Their works were looked upon as the ultimate religious act. Something similar may be meant when our Western tradition speaks of the 'liberal arts', even though this expression did not originally refer to the visual arts. The term may, however, have implied the spiritual area within which perception is possible in free contact with reality, the area within which man becomes freely responsible, free to answer the outside world with his reason, to occupy the position of counterpart to the outer world, which becomes the mirror of his own soul. The Humanists may have meant by 'culture' the ability of man's reason to confront the multiple images of the external world freely, to rediscover the outside image within the human mind and finally transform the orbis into the orbis pictus *so as to be able in turn to confront the external* orbis *in the* orbis pictus. *The 'liberal arts' were also strictly differentiated from everything in the nature of a craft subservient to ends limited by time and space. The more limited and categorized learning became, the more it either led to an abstract world-picture or served more everyday needs, the assurance of a livelihood or technical progress, the more the expression 'liberal arts' came to be restricted to the 'pure' arts—the disinterested activities in which Western man has again and again sought freedom and self-exposure to the world about him.*

Human history begins with the independence of the individual, with the question and the search for an answer; with the question which again and again implies a calling in question, the destruction of accepted ideas and world-pictures—in a word, revolution; the question that both cost Socrates his life and made it of such value. The inexhaustibly fertile West is not to be identified with any one of the forms to which it gave birth; it is neither Baroque nor Romanesque nor Gothic, neither Byzantium nor Rome; in the last analysis it is always the individual, the possibility of individuation, of ever-new departures. Just as the basis of the arts lies in the crafts, so the various historical periods, as opposed to the Western world as a whole, may be looked upon as a necessary precondition for the encounter with reality, as the soil which had to be there before any building could take place at all and which provided the foundation for all questioning and all confrontation with the visual world. Within the various historical periods men were led by tradition to achieve form and to find their own way of dealing with their visual environment. In our own day, however, the West seemed as though it had devoured itself, become infertile, devoid of culture, no longer productive of any personal form, taken off its guard by machine-made interpretations of the world. Then questioning—looking, seeking and answering—reappeared with pristine vigour in art, the domain of human life most closely bound up with the senses. Questions were put with absolute directness, yet astonishingly enough the wealth of tradition, which had seemed to be buried under the rubble of the ages, clearly re-emerged in the work of artists.

Oskar Kokoschka is a figure of our epoch, an epoch apparently doomed to decay, and yet he bears witness in his work to the fertility, the living continuity of the Western world. Rilke wrote of him in a letter: 'It seems as if his great gifts are inseparably bound up with inherent dangers that are perhaps nothing but the universal perils of the age, except that in this artist they are reborn, grow with his artistic output and expand their destructive power in step with the enlargement of his personality.' This same 'destructive power', however, becomes fruitful and productive when harnessed to the work of art. The history of art is a process of breaking down finite form and striving to give concrete shape to infinite reality. It is a story of great individuals; it begins with the Greeks, now almost beyond our understanding, who conceived the human figure in motion, and goes on to the masters of the Byzantine frescoes, to the

9

early French miniaturists, to the creator of the statues at Chartres, to Leonardo, who recognized the movements of light and shade as factors of our vision, to Breughel and Rembrandt, Corot and Delacroix. Kokoschka and his work take their place in this list of masters whose achievements transcended the limitations of their age and so remain for ever vital and timeless. Disregarding the perils involved, he pushes on to the limits of the visually possible, and so overcomes in his work, both as a painter and as a painter committed to the present day, the dangers that threaten him and all of us in this age. Thomas Mann writes in a letter that Kokoschka seems to him the 'epitome of modern painting'. He continues: 'Shall I reduce what I mean to a brief, almost humorous formula? What seems to me to be embodied in Kokoschka's pictures is something like civilized magic. Here is a modern creative spirit who remains true to the phase of evolution in which life has set him down, who shows no trace of the snobbery that is continually looking backwards, no trace of undignified yearning for the primitive, and yet learns to see by the simple process of looking; an initiate, in spite of and along with all his high culture, which he makes no attempt to deny, and in spite of his fin de siècle refinement of taste; an efficient dreamer, a master of precise fantasy, in whose magical work nature and reality become transparent and allow the spirit to shine through.'

PEGASUS
pen and ink, 1951

KOKOSCHKA'S LIFE AND WORK

OSKAR KOKOSCHKA was born on 1 March 1886 in the little town of Pöchlarn on the Danube, the 'Pechelaren' of the *Nibelungenlied*. His father was descended from an old patrician family of Prague goldsmiths, a family in which the humanistic cultural heritage and a tradition of true artistic crafts-manship were kept alive and cultivated. Kokoschka's grandfather, whose jewellery shop was one of the most important in Prague, had taken part in the restoration of the chapel of St Wenceslas on the Hradčany hill and of the imperial crown jewels, and was friendly with the most eminent Czech artists of his day, men like Smetana and Manes; a portrait of Kokoschka's grandmother by Manes is still extant. Kokoschka's mother was the daughter of a forester from Styria, which was then still trackless and thickly wooded. Though she grew up among a large number of brothers and sisters, far from civilization and in wild and exciting surroundings, she had at an early age and on her own initiative acquired profound culture. She was notable for an alert and sensitive mind and the gift of so-called 'second-sight'.

Moulded by a noble craft and the consciousness of a rich tradition, Kokoschka's father, who had come to Lower Austria as a goldsmith in his youth, found it hard to adapt himself to the advance of industrialization and mass-production. In him a powerful urge to economic and intellectual independence was combined with a very limited capacity for business. Hence at the time of Kokoschka's early childhood the family lived an insecure and outwardly poverty-stricken existence, until they moved to a then still rural suburb of Vienna. Here the artist spent his childhood and youth. Vienna was bursting with inner and outer life, the metropolis of a great supra-national empire in which the baroque consciousness of a universal monarchy lived on as an offshoot of the Roman idea of the State and at the same time consumed itself in *fin de siècle* decadent sensuality, hair-splitting intellectualism and crude self-confidence—a fertile soil which produced vital contributions to the intellectual cultural and economic development of the whole of world history. The components of the spiritual atmosphere that fashioned the 'Viennese' were self-confidence and sensitive scepticism, the age-old civilization and undimmed naturalness of border peoples, and a strictly hierarchic ideal of the State and all organization, coupled with intense individualism.

Kokoschka underwent two vitally important experiences during his fifth year: the deaths of his elder brother and a neighbour of whom the boy was fond; she fell to her death through the rotten cover of a well. 'She was going to show me a potted plant in the window which she called *belle de nuit*. This plant was grown in a pot containing a child's skull' (the autobiography of his early life). Around the same period Kokoschka saw his first picture-book: a book on Greek myths, the illustrations to which he coloured in. 'By this means the pictures acquired the scent and taste of honey, which have remained inseparably connected with the Greek myths whenever I think of them.' In his earliest childhood, when he could still scarcely read, his father made him a present of the educational children's book *Orbis Pictus* by the great Czech humanist Jan Amos Comenius. The book exercised an early influence on the child's mind, and throughout his life Kokoschka has revered Comenius as the great master and has striven to put into practice his humanist educational ideals.

After attending a 'modern' school, Kokoschka really intended to study chemistry, attracted by the prospect of investigating the mysteries of matter, the intermingling and interpenetration, attraction and repulsion of the elements. A benevolent teacher, however, who had detected his pupil's marked gift for drawing, obtained a scholarship for him at the Vienna School of Arts and Crafts. Kokoschka, who would otherwise have lacked the financial means to study, planned to utilize this scholarship to pursue his inclinations, still harbouring the idea of becoming a chemist.

Kokoschka's vocation as an artist was not at all clear during his formative years. To be sure, he was considered at school a competent and imaginative draughtsman, and he had also staged a school play, but very few drawings from this period have survived. It seems that drawing was only one of

12

SNAKE DANCE
pen and ink, *c.* 1908

ILLUSTRATION FOR 'MÖRDER, HOFFNUNG DER FRAUEN',
ink, brush and pen, 1908

his means of entering into an intense relationship with the outer world. His strongest and most decisive artistic experiences as a child were derived from the museums of this city with their many art treasures, which became a passion with him at an early age. These experiences did not only come to him in Vienna's big galleries, where he was impressed by the solemn, silent and dusty accumulation of paintings and sculptures, but far more from the well-stocked ethnological collections, which then led a neglected existence as an appendage to the great imperial natural history collection. He was captivated by the powerful expression and strong colours of the masks and fetishes from the South Seas and Africa. Thus he relates that his favourite object was a mask from Neu-Mecklenburg (now New Ireland), the face of which was criss-crossed by a strange nerve-like network of blue lines and decorated with shells and shark's teeth. The forceful and direct artistic impression moved him more than the bloodless classical aesthetic system of ornament he met at the art school. Equally powerful in its effect was his continual contact with the frescoes in Vienna's baroque churches. Maulpertsch, Gran and Kremser-Schmidt were the men from whom Kokoschka first learnt to see and paint; in their pictures infinite space and turbulent life were embodied in a plenitude of colours and

movement. Not until after he left the art school did Kokoschka encounter contemporary painting in a large exhibition of the works of Anton Romako. This important nineteenth-century master, whose work was scarcely known outside the sphere of the Austro-Hungarian monarchy, combines a sensitive Impressionist technique with the dramatic quality and wealth of colour of Baroque. His work has a powerful but restrained pathos that never disrupts the intimacy and neatness of the composition. Romako's pictures, the surface of which often looks like a fragile, tender, nacreous skin, arouse excitement by their realistic expression and their magical atmosphere and depth. They must have been a decisive influence as Kokoschka made his way towards art.

Many threads may have run together to form the knot that constituted the moment of destiny when Kokoschka became a painter. Yet when we consider Kokoschka's personality and work we cannot fail to be struck by the apparent suddenness of this moment. Kokoschka may consciously have decided to become a painter, or he may almost have drifted into it. Anyhow, he began to paint, and from the outset, irrespective of all traceable influences, all technical or formal features he may have adopted from the others, he was entirely himself and his pictures were unmistakable. Completely the child of his age, he nevertheless confronted its influences with supreme self-confidence; he took over a great deal from it, but he transformed and thereby transcended what he took over. No period, no place, no school and no influence could have been more helpful to him than those which actually formed him; yet he, whose work seems to be the ripe fruit of an epoch, presented his epoch with something like an entirely new blossom.

The auspices under which he began his years of study were abundant and favourable; it was one of those moments at which, in a given place, everything was ready for the birth of something of decisive importance. It needed only the spark to start the fire, the last drop to make the vessel over-flow. Looking back we can see how vital in every respect those ten years before the First World War were to the present century, and perhaps to an even longer period. This was particularly so in Vienna, and, as regards the visual arts, especially in the school which Kokoschka entered at the age of nineteen.

WOMAN ROLLER-SKATING
pen and ink, 1909

The official art world of Vienna was still dominated by nineteenth-century academicism and historicism. Not only at the Academy, but also at the School of Arts and Crafts, it was the practice to set the student in front of cold, inert plaster casts of classical sculptures in order to inculcate a feeling for form. Bearded men draped in sheets and leaning on a spear for hours on end in a motionless pose served as models for life drawing. The precise drawing of drapery, modelled with laborious shading, was regarded as the essential prerequisite, particularly for the teaching profession, which Kokoschka had to prepare for under the terms of his scholarship. Nevertheless the decisive break-through to the liberation of line and colour as media of expression had already taken place and had found important champions precisely in the Vienna School of Arts and Crafts. Its principal teachers during this period were Kolo Moser and the stage designer Alfred Roller, both of them pupils of Gustav Klimt, who was the leading figure in the progressive art world of Vienna. There were also close connexions between the School of Arts and Crafts and the Wiener Werkstätte, founded and directed by the eminent architect Josef Hoffmann. Ever since the baroque period Vienna had set the international tone in matters of taste, and Viennese handicrafts had occupied a leading position alongside those to be seen in the Paris *salons*. The Austrian painter Hans Makart had given his name to the Makart bouquet, a dusty construction of ostrich and peacock feathers that was positively a symbol of the upper-middle-class life of the period and, with artistically draped plush curtains and fake armour, formed the inevitable backcloth to every *salon*. But it was also in Vienna that the break-through of *art nouveau* took place, the secession style that represented a turning away from historicism towards truth to material and demanded a new departure in art and crafts in keeping with modern life. The Viennese architect Otto Wagner had taken the crucial step towards modernity; out of his school came Olbrich, who built the Darmstadt Wedding Tower, and Josef Hoffman, whose Palais Stoclet in Brussels is one of the major works of modern architecture. In painting the new movement had discovered the independent value of line and colour as opposed to naturalism and historicism. *Art nouveau* derived considerable impetus from Britain, from William Morris and his disciple Aubrey Beardsley, whose drawings contributed materially to the development of the new style. Contact with Hodler's symbolism was also of vital importance in Vienna. Gustav Klimt, a man of outstanding sensitivity and artistic originality, was the centre of the movement.

At the beginning of his artistic career Gustav Klimt was completely committed to the post-baroque tradition of Makart. He was an excellent and subtle draughtsman, and he and his brother Ernst were among the most sought-after decorative artists of the day. As such he painted bombastic frescoes, among other places in the Burgtheater and the Kunsthistorisches Museum in Vienna, in the Empress Elisabeth's Hermes Villa at Mainz and in many buildings connected with the reigning monarchy. But after his brother's death and a quarrel with the Viennese artists' union he made a radical break with traditional styles, proving himself a strong enough personality to undergo a metamorphosis. He was one of the founders of the Vienna Secession in 1897 and its first president. But in 1905, the year Kokoschka entered the Vienna School of Arts and Crafts, Klimt left the Secession and gathered around him, under the significant title *Ver Sacrum*, 'Sacred Spring', everyone striving for a contemporary mode of expression in the arts. Klimt had a great regard for the initiators of his style—Moreau, Beardsley and Klinger—but he succeeded in passing beyond the symbolic and decorative to a more direct expression. In 1900 Klimt had been commissioned to execute some large ceiling paintings for the assembly hall of the New Vienna University. *Philosophy* was awarded the Grand Prix at the Universal Exhibition in Paris that year but was rejected on aesthetic grounds by the authorities; *Medicine* was similarly rejected on moral grounds. Portraits of women and subtly erotic life-paintings reflected the luxurious and decadent age. Klimt was the portraitist of smart Viennese women. His style is characterized by a delight in costly materials and subtle surfaces accompanied by a sensitive and vital brush-stroke. His influence on the younger generation was strong and fruitful. Klimt had set colour and the brush-stroke free to achieve a direct expressive effect, which made possible Kokoschka's so-called 'Viennese Early Expressionism'. Through his technical brilliance Klimt served as the bearer of a tradition of genuine craftsmanship. In his masterly and generous artistic personality he set the younger men a fine example.

The names of Rilke and Hofmannsthal, Freud and Adler, Musil and Schönberg, Karl Kraus and Franz Werfel must also be mentioned as characteristic of the intellectual atmosphere of Vienna before the First World War, while Georg Trakl and Franz Kafka also belonged within this orbit. Powerful new departures coupled with instability marked this era; the solid structure of tradition had

ADOLF LOOS

ink, brush and pen, *c.* 1909

'Adolf Loos built from within outwards. He occupied no public teaching post, no sinecure created by the State and paid for out of taxes in recognition of his value to the community; neither the Monarchy nor the Republic gave him any honorary title; he obtained his trade certificate as a bricklayer in America in his youth.'

Kokoschka, *Adolf Loos zum Gedächtnis*

KARL KRAUS

ink, brush and pen, *c.* 1909

'Kokoschka made a portrait of me. It is quite possible that those who know me won't recognize me. But I'm quite sure those who don't know me will recognize me.'

Karl Kraus, *Die Fackel*, 9.4.1910

PETER BAUM, 1910
Oil on canvas, $25\frac{5}{8} \times 18\frac{1}{8}$, HMW 43
Wiesbaden, private collection

become shaky and a new and stricter sense of form was making its appearance. In every phase of life there was a search for forms possessing a new immediacy. At the same time blatant social tensions emerged and demanded a sense of responsibility. A period of decadence had aroused extreme sensibility and extreme scepticism. The insecurity of human relationships was such that it could no longer be supported by social forms that first became empty and then impotent.

All this created the hazardous, but also fertile, soil in which Kokoschka's artistic development was nourished.

Oskar Kokoschka seems to have been a very independent-minded, though apt, student at the art school. Dissatisfied with the motionless life models, he demanded and was given an opportunity of working from models in movement. He sought to capture direct impressions in five-minute sketches. Under the influence of Klimt and Čizek, who as a teacher of drawing had discovered child art, the ambitious student acquired a marked talent for sensitive drawing. Little remains from this earliest period of his work. The drawings exhibit firm outlines that break up the surface of the paper into flat areas. The joints are emphasized, and limbs, especially the hands, are fine, elongated and expressive. Hodler's influence is clearly visible in the elongated figures. Kokoschka seems to have drawn a great deal with pen and ink, thus depriving himself of the possibility of making corrections.

Under the influence of a Van Gogh exhibition in Vienna in 1906 Kokoschka began to paint. One of his earliest paintings, a still-life—of which he must have painted many around this time—opens the series of plates in this volume. Highly coloured fruits look like jewels set in the surface of

19

the painting; much is still uncertainly and inexpressively painted, yet the picture as a whole possesses a powerful aesthetic, almost sumptuous charm and gives full evidence of the great colourist Kokoschka was to become. It offers an interesting contrast with a portrait from the same period (*Old Man*, page 47). Here the painter seems to be consciously sacrificing aesthetic to expressive values, as though he wished to free himself from the beautifully painted surface of Klimt and his pupils. This portrait of an old man seems almost to have been painted by an amateur who is striving for the most powerful expression without the necessary artistic technique with which to achieve it. The canvas is densely painted, the colours are hard and in many cases indefinable, while the drawing is crude, forcibly built up or cut in. The contours of the figure are emphasized by the lightness of the background. The pictorial construction is typical of many subsequent portraits. The struggle to portray the 'inner face' has begun. With this picture Kokoschka introduces the long series of portraits in which he makes visible the spiritual landscape of our age and reveals man's exposure to his environment. Whereas with Klimt the spiritual aspect of his sitters is depicted as elegant and light-hearted, in Kokoschka we see the spirit painfully enmeshed and forced to question and cry out.

In the course of these years Kokoschka was taken on by the Wiener Werkstätte. This centre of Viennese taste had initiated the endeavour to achieve modernity in the handicrafts; in it were created the elegant and cultivated fittings and decorations in solid and costly materials that started modern interior decoration. Similar activities were carried on later by the Deutsche Werkstätten and the Dessauer Bauhaus in Germany. For the Wiener Werkstätte Kokoschka designed postcards and posters and painted fans and the like, in return for a modest salary.

1908 saw the most important artistic event to take place in Vienna prior to the First World War —the Vienna Art Exhibition. Organized by the most eminent Viennese artists—the committee was presided over by Gustav Klimt, Franz Čizek, Carl Moll, Josef Hoffmann and Alfred Roller —and supported by the State, this exhibition presented a broad cross-section of the progressive art world of Austria. It gave Kokoschka his opportunity to exhibit in public. He had designed posters for the exhibition and in Room 14 he showed large-scale designs for Gobelin tapestry executed for the Wiener Werkstätte, together with a piece of sculpture and the picture-book *Die Träumenden Knaben* ('The Dreaming Boys'), published by the Wiener Werkstätte press. These uninhibited first works caused a public scandal. The majority of his colleagues and the public were agreed in furiously attacking Kokoschka, but a few critics recognized his importance, among them Ludwig Hevesi, who wrote: 'The arch-barbarian is called Kokoschka, and much is expected of him at the Wiener Werkstätte. This institution has published a book of fairy-tales by him, but it is not for the children of Philistines. Kokoschka is a handsome young man and a gifted fanatic; he will be torn to shreds for his three wall-size sketches for Gobelin tapestries for a ballroom . . . He is also exhibiting a piece of sculpture that will not be bought for the Modern Gallery.' J. A. Lux described him in *Deutsche Kunst und Dekoration* as the 'infant prodigy of the exhibition'; the colourful intoxication of Kokoschka's 'legend of puberty' reminded him of Rimbaud's early poems. Kokoschka's first dramatic work, *Mörder, Hoffnung der Frauen* ('Murderer, Hope of Women'), the origin of German stage Expressionism, was performed in the exhibition's open-air theatre. This performance completed his reputation as an *enfant terrible*. His mechanical 'shadow play' *Das Getüpfte Ei* ('The Spotted Egg') was performed in the *Fledermaus*, the Wiener Werkstätte cabaret in the Kärntner Strasse; figures cut out of tin moved in a lighted box and were made visible to the public with the aid of a mirror.

None of Kokoschka's work shown at the exhibition has survived except *Die Träumenden Knaben*. This was produced in response to a commission from the Wiener Werkstätte for a child's picture-book. The result, however, was something quite different: a picture-book of high merit both as

SELF-PORTRAIT
brush and ink, 1911

21

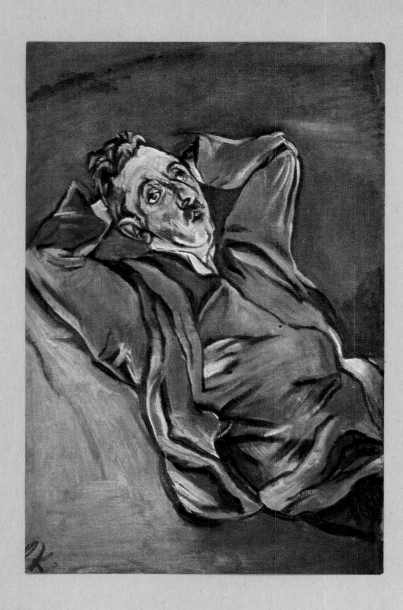

ALBERT EHRENSTEIN, 1914
Oil on canvas, 47¼ × 31½, HMW 90
Prague, Nationalgalerie

literature and from the point of view of the bibliophile. The dream-world of yearnings and fears experienced by the boy in puberty is given direct, at times lyrically tender, at times brutally tormented, expression. The language is here the more advanced, more expressive element. The accompanying pictures—though it is hard to say whether the pictures accompany the words or vice versa—are still entirely under the influence of *art nouveau* in their flowerlike effect and flat areas of colour. The poem, an early twentieth-century literary and artistic masterpiece, was originally published in a very limited edition; it has only recently become generally available again in a small volume issued by the Verlag Galerie Welz, Salzburg. In the whole of his literary output—which occupies a similar position in the history of literature to that held by his paintings in the history of art—as in his pictures, Kokoschka aims at a direct expression of the predicament of the epoch and of mankind as a whole through the themes of unreleased sexuality, hopeless tragedy and decay. Through the destruction of syntax and logical structure language is reduced to a cry and yet retains a lyrical intensity.

At the Vienna Art Exhibition Kokoschka was discovered by Adolph Loos. 'He had designed the posters for the exhibition. I was told that he was an employee of the Wiener Werkstätte and that he was kept busy producing decorated fans, picture postcards and similar examples of the German practice of placing art at the service of the businessman. It was immediately clear to me that one of the greatest sins against the Holy Ghost was here being committed. I sent for him . . .' Loos was one of the period's most awake and awakening spirits. As an architect he was one of the pioneers of the modern functional style. Significantly enough, he entitled one of his trail-blazing essays 'Ornament and Crime'. He turned radically against the history-worshipping secessionist 'cult of the

KARIN MICHAELIS
pen and ink, 1911
   'I packed, he drew. When I bent down, he crawled about on the floor so as
not to let my face out of his sight. The picture was finished in twenty minutes—
but what a picture! Three months' imprisonment would not have been too much
for the resulting "defamation of character". You see, the drawing was published
in *Sturm* . . .'

                Karin Michaelis, *Sturm*, December 1911

SKETCH FOR 'LOVERS WITH CAT'
brush and ink, 1917

façade' and developed his buildings from within, from the lay-out of the rooms. He was closely connected with the literary circle formed around Karl Kraus, Peter Altenberg and Ludwig von Ficker, publisher of the *Brenner* and discoverer and patron of Georg Trakl. Into this circle Loos introduced Kokoschka—after first seeing that he had decent clothes to wear. He drew him away from the Wiener Werkstätte and the School of Arts and Crafts and promised him at least the same income from free-lance work; for this reason he set about obtaining portrait commissions for Kokoschka.

This was the period of the illustrations to *Mörder, Hoffnung der Frauen.* In an intense effort to achieve spatial and psychological depth, the drawing becomes freer. Finely ramified drawing plunges like roots into the interior depths of the figures. The desire to create a spatial conception of the faces is expressed in the superimposition of various views. In *Mörder, Hoffnung der Fauen* we find profile and full-face combined for the first time.

Kokoschka now expressed himself primarily in the portrait, painting the famous pictures of Kraus I, Altenberg, Lotte Franzos and Ebenstein. Merely hinting at the inessential by means of blurred contours, he placed emphatic accent on those parts of the face and hands that are of particular expressive value. He strove to give his models typical poses, laying increasing stress on the typical within the individual. His paintings of this period are rich in tone values but have few strong colours. Over most of the surface the paint is laid on evenly, but in the impasto passages the surface is drawn together by the irregular application of colour.

Unlike the young painters of the Brücke group he was not given to strident self-assertion. There is, rather, something hesitant and groping in the way Kokoschka seeks a method of painting suited to the particular subject. One important painting from this period is the portrait of the children of his friend the bookseller Dr Stein (*Children Playing,* page 49), while the large still-life with the skinned sheep (*Still-Life with Sheep and Hyacinth,* page 51) is quite unique. This picture shows a carcass in front of which there is an empty jug and a creeping tortoise; in the foreground a white mouse is running away and a colourless newt floating in a glass vessel in front of which a ripe fruit is almost bursting

LOVERS WITH CAT, 1917
Oil on canvas, 36⅝ × 51⅛, HMW 116
Zürich, Kunsthaus

with redness; in the right-hand corner stands a ghostly white hyacinth. With its shimmering surface, overflowing with disgust and world-weariness and yet beautiful—all the pictures Kokoschka paints are beautiful, as though in secret agreement with the beauty that is behind everything, which remains in spite of all destruction, all penetration of the crumbling façade—this picture reveals the true face of its whole era. It recalls the mysterious poems of Georg Trakl.

Adolf Loos sent Kokoschka to Switzerland, where his wife had gone for a cure. Kokoschka was received by August Forel, the great biologist, who wished him to paint his portrait. 'After a while Kokoschka painted the picture almost at one stroke, and in the following manner. Forel was sitting at a desk by the window. Kokoschka sat behind his back in the corner of the room and painted Forel as though he were looking at him from the left side. Forel declared: "He must have painted me from memory and feeling, for he couldn't see my face." According to Frau Braun-Forel Kokoschka painted almost the whole picture with his hands and scratched the hair into the thin layer of paint!' (Karl Gruber) But the family wouldn't buy the picture, saying it didn't look like Father, who 'hadn't such dead eyes or such cramped hands.' 'About three years after this picture was painted Forel suffered an apoplectic fit as a result of overstrain at the microscope . . . When Forel's family saw the picture again later they could not deny its great expressiveness and had to admit that it portrayed the essence—the soul—of this strange man.' (Karl Gruber) Kokoschka's intuitive understanding of personality had already shown itself earlier: he had painted a picture of a child and its parents' hands; contrary to reality, the mother's hands appeared unnaturally thick at one point; investigation proved that the woman had actually broken her fingers at this point during her child-hood. His stay in Switzerland was particularly important to Kokoschka on account of the over-whelming impression made upon him by the mountain landscape, to which we owe a magnificent painting of the Dent du Midi.

Loos also brought Kokoschka into contact with Herwarth Walden, the founder and editor of the Berlin periodical *Sturm*. Walden immediately persuaded Kokoschka to come to Berlin as a contributor. Thereafter a series of famous portrait drawings and drawings from the variety stage

NUDE AT TABLE
pen and ink, *c.* 1917

RECLINING CHILD
lithograph, 1917

ILLUSTRATIONS FOR DIRSZTHAY'S
LOB DES HOHEN VERSTANDES,
lithographs, 1917

appeared in *Sturm*, among them *Woman Roller-Skating* and various portraits of the variety artist Goodale. The illustrations to *Mörder, Hoffnung der Frauen* were first printed in *Sturm* and exercised a great influence on later illustrators and stage-designers. The same year, 1910, saw the beginning of Kokoschka's contact with the Berlin art-dealer Cassirer, who initially undertook to buy one picture a year from him. Cassirer started by commissioning a portrait of the actress Tilla Durieux. The majority of portraits belonging to this period, chiefly of members of the *Sturm* circle—Walden, Blümer, Baum, Caro—show an aggressive insistence upon individual characteristics, which are so stressed as almost to amount to caricature. Similarly, the graphic elements of the picture occupy a primary position. Outline and interior drawing stand out black against the even background that is laid on almost like watercolour. The hair and the lines of the face are scratched into the paint with the brush-handle or fingernails, often laying bare the canvas. There are only a few accentuated areas of colour, yet there are already signs of transition to the later so-called 'opaque' period. Such signs are the stippled hair and more hectic colouring of the face in the portrait of the lawyer Caro (page 55). The same development is even more evident in the contemporaneous oil sketch of a cat, where the rich and balanced colours are just as important as the drawing (page 53).

Through his contributions to *Sturm*—which with its distribution of thirty thousand copies was a successful pioneer of, and forum for, the advanced artistic trends of the day—and also through exhibitions at Cassirer's gallery in Berlin and the Folkwang Museum at Hagen, Kokoschka had by this time achieved fairly widespread fame. *Sturm* was one of the most important crystallization points of artistic life in Europe. The leading figures of German Expressionism were gathered round Herwarth Walden, the Blaue Reiter group had its home with him, and he was responsible for the first exhibitions of Chagall and also of Picasso. Nevertheless he was short of money and Kokoschka's first stay in Berlin was a time of grinding poverty, an account of which is given in his *Geschichte von der Tochter Virginia* ('Story of the Daughter Virginia').

STUDY FOR 'WOMAN IN BLUE'
pen and ink, 1919

In the spring of 1911 Kokoschka returned to Vienna. He took on a position as assistant teacher in the Vienna School of Arts and Crafts, where he gave evening life-classes; however, his methods aroused little enthusiasm in his students, most of whom had academic ambitions. One reason for his return may have been the big exhibition in the Hagenbund, in which twenty-five of his paintings were shown. The exhibition aroused savage criticism. Typical of its reception by the public is Archduke Franz Ferdinand's comment: 'The fellow should have every bone in his body broken!' Josef Strzygowski, one of the best known Austrian art critics, called Kokoschka a 'shabby creature' and his pictures 'unappetising ulcers'. On the other hand the cudgels were vigorously taken up on his behalf by Else Lasker-Schüler in the *Sturm* and by Karl Kraus and F. Grüner in the *Fackel*.

Kokoschka now developed a fruitful friendship with Alma Mahler, a woman famed for her beauty and intelligence. She was the wife of the celebrated composer Gustav Mahler and her position in Viennese society was comparable to that of the great women of the Renaissance; her *salon* was frequented by political personalities and financial magnates, men of letters, artists and scientists. Later, after a brief marriage to the director of the Bauhaus, the architect Gropius, she married the poet and novelist Franz Werfel. A strange friendship evolved between the poor painter Kokoschka and the great society lady; the very things which they had in common, and which bound these two strong personalities together, were the source of tremendous tensions and conflicts. This friendship, full of attraction and repulsion, lasted four years. During this period portraits of Alma Mahler, alone or together with him, appear frequently in Kokoschka's work.

Kokoschka's endeavour to rid the picture of its thematic element and to express himself more directly in paint now becomes more clearly manifest. Contours dissolve, colour becomes more

STUDY FOR 'WOMAN IN BLUE'
pen and ink, 1919

independent. This trend is already visible in the portrait of Else Kupfer from the preceding period. Alongside the first portrait of Hermann Schwarzwald, dark-toned but already very painterly in feeling and manifesting a new sense of space, we see the portraits of Baron Dirszthay and Jacques de Menasse, whose brighter, even treatment of colour had been heralded in many of the Berlin pictures.

The 'opaque' period displays Kokoschka's aesthetic metamorphosis, especially in the various pictures with a religious theme. The contours acquire colour; the whole picture is criss-crossed by a network of coloured lines and areas with which the figures are, so to speak, interwoven. The thinly and evenly painted surfaces have a nacreous, iridescent look. The strangely delicate colours create an almost feminine impression of sweetness quite contrary to Kokoschka's usual forcefully masculine style. During this almost mannered period Kokoschka is very much concerned with the craft of painting, applying his pigments in such a way as to produce a surface resembling enamel. This tendency is accompanied by an increasingly strenuous effort to achieve a sense of space by giving the pictures a crystalline structure. Kokoschka is said to have made a practice of observing objects through a crystal while drawing, in order to represent space by refraction into flat planes in a manner analogous to that of the Cubists of the same period.

In 1912 Kokoschka delivered an important lecture to the Academic Association for Literature and Music in Vienna. As Eugenie Schwarzwald tells us, his friends were at first surprised that the apparently taciturn and ineloquent Kokoschka should entertain such a plan. 'Kokoschka then put forward a multitude of unprecedentedly profound ideas about colour, love and art to an audience silent with interest.' In this first lecture on the 'nature of vision' he made an important statement

29

SEATED WOMAN
brush and ink *c.* 1920

regarding the 'consciousness of things seen,' the identity of inner and outer world in vision, a statement to which the painter remained for ever faithful. 'The consciousness of things seen is not a state in which one recognizes or accepts things, but a state in which consciousness experiences itself . . . consciousness lives without bounds, merged and interwoven into things seen. Thus it shares with being all the qualities of life . . . Consciousness is the cause of all things, including conceptions; it is a sea whose horizons are things seen! . . . Consciousness is the grave of things, the point at which they come to an end, the beyond in which they perish. So that as they end they seem no longer to consist of anything more existent than my vision within myself . . . Things will come to act on my behalf and admit themselves of their own accord; I have spoken in your stead with my vision. My spirit has spoken!'

STUDY FOR 'WOMAN IN BLUE'
pen and ink, 1919

At this period Kokoschka seems to have gained a new understanding of himself as a painter, and emerged into a new maturity. In 1913, on a trip to Italy, he came into contact with the works of the great Venetian colourists, above all Tintoretto. On the return journey he produced, in addition to numerous studies for it, the painting of the Dolomite landscape called *Tre Croci* (page 59), a picture in which the spectator is drawn unresisting into a profusion of cool greens, richly toned like exquisite brocade, in which all the colours and all the potentialities of colour are repeated over and over again. The effect is one of infinitely cool, deep pathos.

During the preceding opaque period Kokoschka had learnt to see and paint in colours. He had been through the experience of 'fine painting', of the exquisite quality of pigment. 'The exquisite nature of the craft that makes a gem for the senses out of pigment . . . Colour, which seems nowadays to be undervalued, is not merely a means to an end, not merely a medium for constructing space and not merely a means of expression; it is also an eminently sensuous element that can make the eyes intoxicated as though with exquisite wine . . . the intoxication of radiance. The following story is told of Kokoschka as a child: obsessed by the glitter and glow of fire, the little boy one day thrust his hand into the stove, drew out a piece of burning coal and did not let go of it until it had seared into his hand a scar that remained visible for years.' (Westheim) Kokoschka became a great master in the use of colour as a direct medium of painting. It might be said that he had received the final and greatest initiation into art. Colour is more than a quality of the surface; as matter, it is the ultimate medium of sight as such. Just as, in terms of physics and physiology, colour first comes into existence

31

in the act of seeing, through the impact of light upon the retina, so it is also the factor that links the outer world to the inner. It is at one and the same time the challenge of reality and its answer in the act of vision.

Kokoschka was also a master at keeping colour within bounds. Bright colours are embedded in cool tones. This was the period of his magnificently dramatic portraits of men—of Carl Moll or his friend Albert Ehrenstein, for example. The subjects of the pictures seem to be withdrawn from the spectator, bound up in their own sphere of existence without any direct psychological reference to the spectator. The main work of this period is the large painting in the Basle Museum of Art, *The Bride of the Wind* (page 61). This picture, which is prodigious in its very proportions, constitutes an ecstatic symphony in blue. At the time, Kokoschka was toying with the idea of painting frescoes and he produced something akin to the great symbolic architectural painting of the Baroque. He presents his metaphor in broad, monumental language. The loving couple, who have the features of Kokoschka and Alma Mahler, recline in a boat in the midst of a blue whirlpool, drawn simultaneously towards and apart from one another. Everything is in movement and yet at rest. The cold deep blue and the azure are set in motion by lighter tones and red. The picture radiates an immense depth of experience.

Around this time, at the beginning of 1914, Kokoschka broke with Alma Mahler. He produced one more graphic masterpiece—*The Bach Cantata*—lithographs on the text 'O eternity, thou word of thunder'. The power and tragedy of sexuality, everlasting attraction and repulsion, appear here as an image of the mystery of eternity, as in his literary works. One of the finest self-portraits, which appears in this folio as a lithograph, he subsequently carried out as a painting. His eyes gaze at us with an expression of knowledge and inquiry, his hands wielding the brush are opened as though in a gesture of resignation.

After the outbreak of war Kokoschka volunteered for the Imperial and Royal 15th Dragoons, one of the most aristocratic Austrian cavalry regiments, his admission to which had been arranged by Adolf Loos. After the war had begun and as though he had a premonition of what was to come, Kokoschka painted a shattering picture entitled *The Straying Rider*. The figure lies on a hillock in

THE ARTIST AND THE MUSE
lithograph, 1921

ILLUSTRATION FOR DIRSZTHAY'S
'DER UNENTRINNBARE'
pen and ink, 1923

MARIA ORSKA
lithograph, 1922

front of a wide and turbulent landscape, like something from a painting by Altdorfer, alone, his hands outstretched in a questioning, lamenting, empty gesture. Severely wounded during an attack in Galicia, Kokoschka himself lay like this, and a Russian soldier bent on delivering the *coup de grâce* thrust a bayonet into his chest. Instead of shooting him with the revolver he held in readiness, Kokoschka laughed in the soldier's face. 'He had left his gun sticking into me, it must have fallen over through its own weight; he was the one who was scared, and he ran away. There is an ultimate point beyond which fear is unable to go. Violence is like a rusty key that is turned too far in the lock.' Thus ends the story *Verwundung* ('The Wound'), in which Kokoschka describes this experience.

His inner and outer situation before the war was such that military service may almost have represented deliverance for him. After he had been forced by growing hostility to give up his post as assistant teacher at the School of Arts and Crafts in 1912, Kokoschka had worked for a short time as drawing master at the girls' private school run by the well-known Viennese educationist Eugenie Schwarzwald. But the girls' parents considered that the influence of a young man named in so many artistic scandals must be harmful to their daughters, and the education authorities forbade him to continue teaching in Austrian schools. His friendship with Alma Mahler had also turned into an anguished relationship. He had given her in farewell six magnificent swan-skin fans, on which he had painted symbolic allusions and real memories of their time together.

At the end of 1915 Kokoschka entered a military hospital in Vienna severely wounded by a bullet in the head and a bayonet thrust in the lung. While suffering from depression and feverish delirium he began to write his great drama *Orpheus und Eurydike*, later set to music by Křenek. During his convalescence Kokoschka began to paint again. The unbroken courage of the mortally sick painter is manifest in his portrait of a lady with a parrot (page 63). The beautifully balanced picture, painted with confident strength has the restful yet rich colours of a baroque Gobelin. During this period he met Rilke and Hofmannsthal in Vienna. After a temporary recovery he was sent to the

GIRL WITH FLOWERS IN HER HAIR, *c.* 1930
Oil on canvas, 28⅜ × 23⅝, HMW 158
Prague, private collection

Isonzo front as a war correspondent; but in August 1916 he was finally discharged from military service as unfit.

In the autumn Kokoschka went to Berlin again as the guest and collaborator of Herwarth Walden. Cassirer also renewed his contract with him. In 1917 Kokoschka had to go to Stockholm for a time to receive after-treatment from a specialist for his head wound, as a result of which he was suffering severe disturbance of equilibrium and continual depression. The specialist could do nothing for him, however, and in spite of his condition Kokoschka seriously thought of having himself sent back to the front, in the hope of being killed. But the fervour and vitality of his personality as an artist showed him the way to overcome his difficulties in his work. Through his friend Albert Ehrenstein he made the acquaintance of Dr Fritz Neuberger, who invited him to his little house on the Weisser Hirsch. His house was occupied and visited by several gifted writers and actors, among them Walther Hasenclever, Ivar von Lücken and Ernst Deutsch, whose portraits crop up over and over again among Kokoschka's works of this period.

He was profoundly impressed by the works of the old masters in the Dresden Gallery; Cranach's and Rembrandt's pictures, in particular, served him as stimulating models. He now produced large paintings with an exquisite profusion of colours. There is a great deal of movement in the composition, intended, it would appear, to introduce something of the infinitude of the cosmos into the picture-frame; the restlessly swirling brush-stroke, though it may also be the outcome of the disturbance of the artist's inner and outer equilibrium, seems to serve the same purpose. The chief pictures of this period, *The Emigrant, Lovers with Cat, The Friends* (page 67), deal in an insistent, searching manner

35

GENOA, VIEW OF HARBOUR, 1932–3
Oil on canvas, $31\frac{3}{4} \times 39\frac{1}{4}$
Zürich, private collection

with the theme of human relatedness. They show signs of Kokoschka's efforts to overcome his difficulty in establishing human contacts. In between them comes the large self-portrait (page 65) which, in the hectic colours of this period, shows the painter exposed and solitary and in a pose suggesting that he is both giving an explanation and helplessly questioning. Kokoschka is increasingly concerned to produce painting composed of sweeping strokes and reminiscent of Gobelin tapestry. In order to give a special consistency to his paint, which he now laid on very thickly, he appears to have mixed a heavy, resinous gum with his pigments.

In his despair of ever attaining deeper human relationships, Kokoschka had a life-size doll made to his specifications, which was to serve him as a companion and a model. It inspired numerous paintings and drawings. The most important of these is the *Woman in Blue* (page 69), in which a new development manifests itself. The erratic brush-strokes disappear, the colours are fused into large, monumental areas with broad strokes of the brush or palette knife, graphic elements no longer appear. The large number of studies for this painting is exceptional in Kokoschka's work. He generally works direct on the canvas, and since he frequently takes a long time to complete a picture the different phases through which it passes are superimposed upon one another in layers.

During the year in which he painted *Woman in Blue*, 1919, Kokoschka was appointed to a professorship at the Dresden Academy. He moved into lodgings with Hans Posse, the director of the Dresden Picture Gallery, in a mansion in the Grosser Garten. Here he lived a somewhat retiring life. Working with great concentration he produced in the Academy studio on the Brühl Terrace nine large, harmoniously proportioned views of Dresden and the banks of the Elbe (page 34). The very thick colours are placed side by side as though in a glowing mosaic; the rectangular composition of these pictures, divided by the broad horizontal band of the bank of the Elbe, is also reminiscent of a mosaic and helps to give them a feeling of quietude. In addition to these landscapes Kokoschka painted a number of portraits and pictures with a biblical theme—*Lot and his Daughters*

THE VISIT, 1934
Oil on canvas, 29⅛ × 36¼, HMW 282
Prague, Nationalgalerie

and *Jacob, Rachel and Leah*—in which he sought, with the aid of his newly acquired method of com-
posing purely with colour, to break away from the classical triangular construction of a picture.

Kokoschka's graphic output reached great heights at this period. He produced numerous portrait
lithographs, among them the brilliant cycle *The Concert, Variations on a Theme*, showing six variations
on the portrait of the wife of the eminent Viennese art-historian Max Dvořak. During the last three
years of his stay in Dresden, 1922–4, Kokoschka concentrated mainly on watercolours.

Much has been said about the social conscience which Kokoschka developed while in Dresden;
this led him to give generous financial assistance both to his students and to friends. He devoted
almost the whole of his income to helping those poorer than himself. 'His opposition to injustice
and intolerance and his all-embracing love of children and the poor were part of his deep-feeling
nature . . . Although his students were affectionately attached to him and learnt a great deal from him,
Dresden and his teaching activities did not satisfy his restless spirit for long. He was not made to remain
tied to a place or a task. Like Poelzig he resolutely shook the dust of Dresden from his feet. One day
Kokoschka had vanished without trace, without announcing his departure, without giving notice
and without saying good-bye. He went wandering through Europe and never returned.' (Paul F.
Schmidt)

The period of wandering that followed lasted ten years, till Kokoschka settled in Prague—
though for reasons beyond his control he did not stay there long. In the course of these ten years he
produced a multitude of views of towns and landscapes such as we do not find in the work of any
of the great painters since the end of the baroque period; they constituted Kokoschka's *orbis pictus*,
his painted world. His crucial years of development were past, although even his late work cannot
be described as standing still. Kokoschka's desire to experience the world, with all its great size and
scope, as the home of mankind and to arouse this experience in the depths of the spectator led him to
give his landscapes a look of almost infinite distance. The change in subject-matter and working

LA PASSIONARIA

lithograph, 1937

'The strange title of this lithograph, the Spanish word *La Passionaria*, means "the passion-flower" and was on everyone's lips at that time as the *nom de guerre* of a prominent Republican woman freedom-fighter. Kokoschka did not identify himself with any party. Works like *La Passionaria* are statements of his faith in the guiding principle of charity.'

H. M. Wingler, *Kokoschka-Fibel*

conditions called for a different method of painting. 'The addition of turpentine rendered the pigment more fluid and flexible, so that it could be employed, as if in drawing, to make graphic elements or individual details in the painting stand out more clearly.' (H. M. Wingler)

In the spring of 1924 Kokoschka settled for several months at Blonay on the Lake of Geneva, from where he made visits to Italy. From one of these he brought back his first picture of Venice, *Boats near the Dogana, Venice* (page 73). The death of his father compelled him to stay for a while in Vienna, which he left at the end of the year for Paris. Until 1933 this remained his permanent head-quarters, though he never stayed there for long at a time. In the course of these years long trips financed by his dealer Cassirer took him through Europe, Africa and the Near East. In 1925 he painted a number of landscapes in the South of France and Spain. After this he paid visits to Amsterdam and England. In 1926 Kokoschka painted pictures of animals in the London Zoo, among them *The Tiger-Lion* (page 81). The large Thames landscapes and *Richmond Terrace* (page 83) date from the same year. At the beginning of 1927 Kokoschka painted the picture of *Lyons* (page 89), in which his new system of perspective becomes clearly manifest for the first time. His endeavour to arouse in the spectator the illusion of space led him to turn away from traditional geometric perspective with a single viewpoint. Kokoschka evolved a perspective with two intersecting visual points; this he attributed partly to an inborn astigmatism which he shared with some of the great colourists of the classical period—Titian, El Greco—and of which he became aware through his war wound, or rather through the resulting disturbance of equilibrium. This method of employing two axes produces a 'conception of the world as confined within a sphere.'

After this came Kokoschka's trips to Africa, where for the first time the Arab world made a profound impression on him, which was doubtless why he visited the Near and Middle East—Egypt, Istanbul, Jerusalem—in 1929. This was followed by shorter journeys to Scotland and Ireland. In the intervals Kokoschka always came back to Paris and also paid visits to Vienna and Berlin.

In the course of these years Kokoschka had risen to a position of the first importance among European painters. By this time there existed a large number of publications devoted to his works, and even in France, where all art stemming from the German zone of culture normally met with a very cold reception, he enjoyed universal critical acclaim on the occasion of a big exhibition. His paintings figured in all the larger and more progressive museums and collections, especially, of course, in Germany. His paintings, and also his drawings and studies, won first prizes in competitions. Then came the economic crisis, which so shattered the art market that it became virtually impossible to sell pictures or obtain commissions. The Cassirer Gallery was compelled to terminate its contract with Kokoschka. The latter moved to his little house in the Liebhartstal in Vienna, where the munici-pal council had commissioned him to paint a view of the city. The great view of Vienna from the Wilhelminenberg with children playing (page 97) shows new allegorical tendencies strongly influenced by Breughel. The unusual picture was, for the time being, not accepted by the Vienna municipal council, and in 1932 Kokoschka moved back to Paris. In the midst of this disastrous economic situation Kokoschka painted the *Self-Portrait with Cap* (page 99), which demonstrates his unbroken supremacy as a painter and a man. But economic pressure grew more and more acute, and throughout almost the whole of 1933 Kokoschka stayed with a friend in Rapallo, finally giving up his home in Paris altogether and returning to Vienna.

But political developments in Germany, as well as in Austria, perturbed the libertarian artist; he fled the German-speaking area and made his way to the home of his father—Prague. Here he produced a whole series of Prague urban landscapes, most of them with a view of the Moldau. Flickering light seems to have been shaken out over the landscape in a myriad patches of colour;

CATHLEEN, COUNTESS OF DROGHEDA, 1943–6
Oil on canvas, 40⅛ × 29⅞, HMW 336
London, private collection

the water flashes and glitters in the light like a jewel. There had been many hints of this Impressionist way of painting during the preceding period of his travels. But there can be no doubt that, unlike the Impressionists, Kokoschka projected into these landscapes inner impressions and his relaxed and sovereign attitude towards life. In Prague he was in contact with the then president of the Czechoslovakian Republic, Masaryk, who, like himself, was an adherent of the humanitarian and educational views of Jan Amos Comenius. He painted a portrait of Masaryk accompanied by an ideal likeness of the Moravian educationist. This picture marked a revival of Kokoschka's liking for allegorical and historical subjects, which were to provide him with numerous motifs culminating in the great triptych *Thermopylae*. In Dr Palkovsky's house in Prague he also met his future wife, who provided the theme for several important drawings. In 1937 the exhibition of 'Degenerate Art' was held in Munich, and afterwards four hundred and seventeen of Kokoschka's paintings and drawings in German museums were seized and some of them sold abroad. Under the influence of this news he produced the magnificently critical and alert *Self-Portrait as a Degenerate Artist*.

In 1938 he fled with his future wife, Olda Palkovska, from the ominous situation in Central Europe to England. Having no means of subsistence, he had to look for new means of gaining a livelihood; shortly after the outbreak of war Kokoschka moved with his wife to Polperro in Cornwall; his wife helped to earn a living by selling gastronomic specialities from her homeland. During the

POSTER
lithograph

At Christmas 1945 five thousand copies of this poster were pasted up all over London and other British cities. There was no organization behind this action, which Kokoschka carried out entirely at his own expense. At the same time, as an immigrant to Britain, he published a memorandum calling for tolerance towards the defeated enemy to lay the foundations of a genuine and lasting peace. He wrote at the time in a letter to Dr A. Neumeyer: 'This is not a world with any future, hope or faith . . . I go on working, but I know that it is a lost battle. What keeps me alive is a growing pity for the suffering of innocent children.'

war years Kokoschka painted a great many political-allegorical pictures in protest against the inhumanity of war. In London he painted, among other portraits, such as that of the Soviet ambassador Maisky, the radiantly colourful and supremely confident portrait of Lady Drogheda. Kokoschka was also president of a committee that set itself the task of gathering together the cultural forces still alive in Germany and testifying abroad to their existence. In 1945 he appealed in a deeply moving poster, which he had put up at his own expense, for aid to the suffering children of Europe.

Soon after the war Kokoschka made fresh trips to the Continent to study the lie of the land and draw up a spiritual balance-sheet. Years of wandering followed. In 1947, during a longish stay in Switzerland, he painted a series of Swiss landscapes under the influence of the mountains (pages 107 and 109). The following year his travels took him to America, where he delighted in increasing public recognition and lectured as a visiting professor at Boston University. Kokoschka also reestablished relations with his homeland. He spent a considerable part of 1950 in Salzburg, where he painted a large view of the town (page 111). The first plans were laid for an international summer school at Salzburg, the 'School of Seeing'. These were put into effect, thanks to the initiative of Friedrich Welz and under his administrative direction, in 1953 and the following summers. The same year Kokoschka settled with his wife on the Lake of Geneva, from which base he has made numerous journeys to all parts of the world. But summer after summer he returns to Salzburg, impelled by his educational idea of teaching men to see and to experience the act of seeing by the practice of painting.

Since the war Kokoschka has emerged as the representative painter of his age. He has received numerous portrait commissions, among them portraits of the German and Austrian heads of State. Big cities have requested urban landscapes by his hand, and he has been showered with honours. Nevertheless his endeavour to achieve direct experience remains, every picture is still a hazard, a new creation. Above everything Kokoschka places his humanist ideals; he has championed them in innumerable writings and lectures. He remains a passionate seeker after truth, rousing men to experience this truth with their eyes. His own words in a lecture on Rembrandt, also apply to himself:

'If an artist is capable of looking truth so clearly in the face that, while discerning the transitory, he can yet give it permanent form, can yet render the immortal visible in mortal shape, then he has done more than any words can convey.'

THE PLATES

STILL-LIFE WITH PINEAPPLE 1907

Oil on canvas, 43¼×31½, HMW 3

Berlin, Museum Dahlem (formerly Nationalgalerie)

This is the earliest definitely known painting by Kokoschka. At the age of twenty, while in his first year at the School of Arts and Crafts, he was stimulated to paint by seeing Van Gogh's pictures in an exhibition. Van Gogh's influence is clearly visible in this picture, but Kokoschka has already boldly transcended it in the independent vigour of his handling of colour. In the early literature on Kokoschka this picture is usually attributed to a much later period of his work because of its maturity, but there is absolutely no doubt about its correct dating. One of Kokoschka's teachers at the School of Arts and Crafts, Berthold Löffler, reports seeing another broadly painted still-life by Kokoschka in the autumn of 1907, which was 'very fine' and far more than a beginner's work. This picture subsequently disappeared.

OLD MAN . FATHER HIRSCH 1907

Oil on canvas, 26¾×24, HMW 4

Linz, Neue Galerie der Stadt Linz

This picture is the first in a long series of Kokoschka's portraits. Little is known about the sitter. He is said to be 'Father' Hirsch, an acquaintance of Kokoschka at that time, who occasionally gave him financial assistance. The fruit that served as a model for the still-life with pineapple was a present from him. But confronted by this picture, this terrifying 'life mask', we cannot attach much importance to the personal details of the sitter. It is the portrait of a man in whom, above and beyond the personal element, the artist found something typical—the sign and expression of a situation. Kokoschka's first biographer, Westheim, writes of the period in which this picture was painted: 'He had no ability in the academic sense. Nor was he likely to make any progress in what people call painting, that is to say other people's language. Out of an inner need he had spontaneously to create phonetic symbols that enabled him to utter what happened to be filling his mind.

'This is Kokoschka's way of trying to put a *tabu* upon the human beings who whirr threateningly around him like phantoms of the air. He feels that he must exorcise them by pinning them down, as is the ancient custom in dealing with ghosts. That is to say, he starts drawing and painting them. He tries to lay hold of the disturbing element in them.'

CHILDREN PLAYING 1909

Oil on canvas, $28\frac{3}{4} \times 42\frac{1}{2}$, HMW 19

Duisburg, Museum

The children are those of the Viennese bookseller Dr Stein, who, at a time when Kokoschka's work was still the object of universal hostility and ridicule, also commissioned a portrait of himself. This picture must certainly have been painted prior to Kokoschka's trip to Switzerland; the colours are subservient to the linear, graphic composition, a sign of Hodler's influence, which was very great on Kokoschka's school, but also a sign of Kokoschka's interest in Japanese art. Kokoschka has completely avoided the temptation to paint the kind of 'beautiful' children's portrait in fashion since the Romantic period. The children look gentle and fragile, as though abandoned, deprived of the protection of a safe environment; and yet, despite all the freedom from illusion and the acuteness of observation, they are painted with heartfelt tenderness. The warm, softly flowing tones seem to echo memories of the interiors of Vienna's baroque churches.

STILL-LIFE WITH SHEEP AND HYACINTH 1909

Oil on canvas, $34\frac{1}{4} \times 44\frac{7}{8}$, HMW 21

Vienna, Österreichische Galerie

This picture was painted in the house of the Viennese collector Dr Reichel. Kokoschka was inspired to produce this strange composition by a skinned sheep seen in a butcher's window. The ghostly glimmer of decomposition, of mould and disintegration, here appears strangely attractive and beautiful. Fascinated by nausea, the symbol of decadence, Kokoschka reveals himself in this work as a spiritual brother of the French Symbolists or the Austrian poet Georg Trakl; but in its beauty this picture also points to a higher order of aesthetic life and vision.

CAT (*sketch*) 1910

Oil on canvas, $18\frac{1}{8} \times 27\frac{1}{8}$, HMW 42

Munich, private collection

This picture was probably painted in Berlin while Kokoschka was collaborating with Herwarth Walden on the *Sturm*. In his *Geschichte von der Tochter Virginia* he writes of this period: 'I rarely signed my pictures because at that time I was still ashamed to sell my work; on the final decisive day I always had inhibitions. I often forsook picture and paint-box; the purchase of a new paint-box became a particular problem. I should have liked to solve the puzzle of how to remain an independent artist without starving to death.'

The subtly varied colours of this picture show Kokoschka's evolution towards a purely painterly approach; but the graphic elements are still the essential media of expression. Kokoschka's pictures of animals occupy a unique position in his work at this period. They undoubtedly have symbolic significance. The cat is caught at that tense moment when, having contracted her claws, she may next instant spring into the air or stretch out cosily purring. 'The honest domestic cat here becomes the prototype of the sphinx.' (H. M. Wingler)

HUGO CARO 1910

Oil on canvas, $35 \times 21\frac{5}{8}$, HMW 44

Winterthur, Kunstmuseum

The Berlin lawyer Dr Caro was a friend of Herwarth Walden and his first wife.
In the Berlin portraits of personalities belonging to the *Sturm* circle Kokoschka
stresses individual characteristics to the point of caricature, employing primarily
graphic means. Caro's portrait is one of the most painterly of this period. The
journalist Peter Scher, whose portrait has not survived, describes Kokoschka's
methods of working at this time: 'Then he went to work. He began to scrub
around with the stub of a pencil on a large sheet of ordinary foolscap paper, shading
the drawing with a stump. He also squeezed paint out of the tube and scratched
around in it with his fingernail, commenting that there was no reason why one
should shrink from using even a hammer and a crowbar, for what did "drawing"
and "painting" mean when all that mattered was to produce something convincing?'

FLIGHT INTO EGYPT 1911

Oil on canvas, $21\frac{5}{8} \times 26\frac{3}{4}$, HMW 52

Zürich, private collection

In the spring of 1911 Kokoschka returned from Berlin to Vienna, where he took a post at the School of Arts and Crafts. He entered on his so-called 'opaque' period, in which 'the pigments are fused into a homogeneous, tinted mass of colour over which is drawn a slightly opalescent skin. This shimmering surface becomes the specific quality of the works dating from the beginning of his second Viennese phase.' (H. M. Wingler.) His endeavour to achieve an aesthetically pleasing surface can be seen in a series of paintings on religious themes. In a manner analogous to the contemporaneous Cubist solution of the problem of space, Kokoschka seeks during this period to divide space into planes by giving his pictures a crystalline structure. He is said to have been in the habit of looking at objects through a crystal while drawing at this period.

TRE CROCI, DOLOMITES 1913

Oil on canvas, $32\frac{1}{4} \times 46\frac{7}{8}$, HMW 81

Hamburg, private collection

During a trip to Italy with Alma Mahler in 1913 Kokoschka once again encountered the great Venetian colourists, especially Tintoretto. This picture of the Dolomite pass near Cortina d'Ampezzo was painted on the return journey. 'What broke through with vehemence around 1914, and has remained crucial for the whole of Kokoschka's painting right up to the present, was a mighty, roaring respiration, something that cannot be better described than as a baroque feeling, which filled the pictures sometimes with raging turbulence, sometimes with a vast, tranquil breath.' (F. Schmalenbach)

THE BRIDE OF THE WIND 1914

Oil on canvas, $71\frac{1}{4} \times 86\frac{5}{8}$, HMW 96

Basle, Kunstmuseum

This forceful composition was originally called by Kokoschka *The Big Boat*. The lovers have the features of the artist and Alma Mahler. The painting immortalizes this friendship, which came to an end the year it was produced, and at the same time elevates it to a universal, supra-sensual level. 'The aim in this composition is to express violent movement—the hurricane in nature, the stormy passion of the lovers that is blind to the raging of the elements—entirely by means of colour. The task is to portray movement, great epic ardour, through colour and indeed through a single colour. He seeks to burrow into the surface by varying the manner in which the paint is applied, now opaque, now as a glaze, now so as to create an impression of permanency, now of fleetingness. Resistances are, so to speak, built in so as to increase the amount of power available; the aim is to establish contacts between those currents that circle underground . . . The vision materializes; all at once it is there, this great, mightily billowing blue, the blue a poet like Trakl carried within him in the shape of unappeased yearning.' (P. Westheim)

LADY WITH PARROT 1916

Oil on canvas, $33\frac{1}{8} \times 20\frac{1}{8}$, HMW 108

Berlin, private collection

After being severely wounded and escaping death by the skin of his teeth, Kokoschka entered a Viennese military hospital. During his convalescence he began to paint again. This portrait, painted at this period, is redolent of calm inwardness and pleasure in beauty. The colours are interwoven as in a baroque Gobelin and display a new and deeper joy in the beauty of painting, the exquisite loveliness of colour.

SELF-PORTRAIT 1917

Oil on canvas, $30\frac{3}{4} \times 24\frac{3}{8}$, HMW 115

Wuppertal, private collection

At important moments in his life Kokoschka again and again confronts himself
in the self-portrait, as did Rembrandt, whose works came as a vital experience to
Kokoschka during his stay in Dresden. The thick colours that shimmer like
enamel are set on the canvas with vigorous, jerky brush-strokes, without disturbing
the tranquil composition of the picture as a whole. 'Every stroke in his painting is
intensely personal in its effect. Hence he always comes back to his own ego, which
bears a heavy responsibility for the universal, in which heaven and hell impinge
upon one another,' Paul Westheim wrote of Kokoschka the year this self-portrait
was painted.

THE FRIENDS 1917–18

Oil on canvas, 39⅜×59, HMW 119

Linz, Neue Galerie der Stadt Linz

Kokoschka began to paint this picture at the end of 1917 in Fritz Neuberger's house on the Weisser Hirsch in Dresden; he originally called it *The Gamblers*. It represents the circle of his closest friends at that time: the actress Käthe Richter, the poet Walter Hasenclever, the writer Ivar von Lücken, Dr Fritz Neuberger, Kokoschka himself seen from the rear, and in the background a waitress. In a letter to Hans Tietze, Kokoschka wrote of the picture: 'It shows my friends playing cards. Each terrifyingly naked in his ardour, and all immersed in a scale of colours of a higher order, which binds them together as light elevates an object and its reflection into a category that has something of the real object and something of the reflection and hence more of both of them . . .'

WOMAN IN BLUE 1919
Oil on canvas, $29\frac{1}{2} \times 39\frac{2}{8}$, HMW 126
Stuttgart, Württembergische Staatsgalerie

Kokoschka found a model for a series of drawings and paintings in a life-sized doll made by a craftswoman exactly to his own specifications. This picture is probably identical with the painting called *Mania* shown at the XIIIth Biennale. *Mania* is an anagram of the word *anima* and is meant to describe the sensual female, the seductress as opposed to the mother. Painterly elements come to the fore in this picture, which is laid in with broad strokes of pigment that combine into wide areas; the element of pure drawing has been eliminated. The restless brush-stroke of the preceding paintings has completely vanished; this picture constitutes a transition to the period that follows, in which the composition depends entirely upon the distribution of colours.

DRESDEN, NEW TOWN II 1921
Oil on canvas, $22\frac{7}{8} \times 31\frac{1}{2}$, HMW 135
Detroit, The Detroit Institute of Arts

In a series of views of Dresden the colours look like pieces in a mosaic arranged in a strict, almost rectangular composition of flat areas. Kokoschka painted this picture, like most of his views of the banks of the Elbe, from his studio window. Paul F. Schmidt writes of a visit to Kokoschka's studio at this period: 'The Academy building at the corner of the Brühl Terrace, crowned with a glass dome (which the young artists compared to a lemon-squeezer), looked like a piece of architecture that had gone dramatically wrong. Anyone who went right inside one of the immensely high and wide studios used by the masters was liable to be seized with agoraphobia. The frightful decorations based on a misunderstanding of Baroque had found their way from the façade into the interior, and the use of a quite exceptionally desolate-looking grey paint for the walls completed the impression of being caught in a stone nightmare. Professor Kokoschka also occupied one of these studios . . . There could be no more intense contrast than that between the sumptuous colours of his canvases and their surroundings. They stood out in the gloomy cavern like sparkling jewels, emitting a radiance that triumphed over all earthly misery.'

BOATS NEAR THE DOGANA, VENICE 1924

Oil on canvas, $29\frac{1}{2} \times 37\frac{3}{8}$, HMW 167

Munich, Bayerische Staatsgemäldesammlungen

In 1924 Kokoschka left Dresden and spent several years wandering. During this period he produced a unique series of landscapes and views of towns. Impelled by the desire for a wide vista, he sought the highest possible viewpoint. This, the first of his views of Venice, was painted on a trip from Blonay on the Lake of Geneva. The paint is thin and fluid and is used to convey graphic details; at the same time it is filled with a new free lightness. Kokoschka depicts the world as light and wide, the home of mankind.

MADRID, PUERTA DEL SOL 1925

Oil on canvas, $26\frac{3}{8} \times 38\frac{5}{8}$, HMW 194

Switzerland, private collection

In 1925, starting from Paris, Kokoschka went on a trip to the south of France, Spain and Portugal. In this picture the harsh colours seen in the bright light and dry air of the Iberian peninsula combine with the busy activity of the Spanish capital. An atmospheric impression of this city, which grew up in the nineteenth century, is given with a minimum of reference to the historical aspect embodied in its monuments.

75

LONDON, LARGE THAMES LANDSCAPE I 1926

Oil on canvas, $35\frac{3}{8} \times 51\frac{1}{8}$, HMW 208

Buffalo, Albright Art Gallery

During a stay in London lasting several months, Kokoschka was fascinated by the view across the city cloven by the broad river. From his hotel on the Victoria Embankment, behind Cleopatra's Needle, he painted almost the same view three times: in its morning and evening moods and once again nineteen years later. Here the light breaks through the morning mist in a flood of warm colours and discloses the typical outline of the City.

TIGER-LION 1926

Oil on canvas, $37\frac{3}{4} \times 50\frac{3}{4}$, HMW 216

New York, Museum of Modern Art

During his stay in England in 1926 Kokoschka found in the London Zoo a theme
that is rare in his work. He painted several large pictures of animals that capture
the image of untamed ferocity in swift and vigorous strokes. The remarkable
amalgamation of graphic and painterly elements—streaks and strands of paint
break away from the surface, at once indicating and dissolving the contours and
reaching out into space—emerges even more clearly in later phases of his work.
In his manner of painting we can detect the artist's concentrated eagerness to capture the fleeting image in a picture that is full of spontaneity.

RICHMOND TERRACE 1926

Oil on canvas, $35\frac{3}{8} \times 51\frac{1}{8}$, HMW 218

Zürich, private collection

Kokoschka's first years of travel, and especially his stay in England, were a fruitful period where his work was concerned. The multitude of impressions he received were absorbed, concentrated, and released in his pictures, in which he constantly strove to suit the type of painting to the particular task in hand. The paintings of this period, such as this landscape of the former royal gardens by the Thames at Richmond, are marked by a strongly lyrical mood. 'The solemnity of sunset, the idyllic quality of the park landscape and the sedateness of the old English way of life harmoniously blend in this fabric of festal cobalt and vaporous green, sprinkled with white light and shot through with yellow and a few dark threads.' (H. M. Wingler)

CHAMONIX AND MONT BLANC 1927

Oil on canvas, $35\frac{3}{8} \times 51\frac{1}{8}$, HMW 230

Küssnacht, private collection

While travelling from Venice through the south of France to Paris, Kokoschka was once again impressed by the majestic might of the Swiss Alps. Since the huge pieces of mountain architecture in Altdorfer's paintings this subject had scarcely been dealt with in painting. Eschewing petty detail or formless pathos, Kokoschka has captured an impression of overwhelming grandeur in a powerful play of colour and light.

LAC D'ANNECY I 1927

Oil on canvas, $27\frac{5}{8} \times 35\frac{7}{8}$, HMW 231

Santa Barbara (California), private collection

The blue that recurs again and again, in an infinite variety of tones, as the colour of distant water and air is a basic colour-theme in Kokoschka's paintings. The landscapes of this period are almost always painted in the soft radiance of morning or evening. Yet the great respiration of nature that can be felt in these pictures never overwhelms the human element. Man and nature, civilization and landscape are not in opposition; everything seems to be seen as one great, peaceful homeland.

LYONS 1927

Oil on canvas, $38\frac{1}{8} \times 51\frac{1}{8}$, HMW 232

Washington, Phillips Memorial Gallery

Round the citadel crowned by the church of Notre-Dame de Fourvière the Saône winds its way into the far background, towards the sea. In order to give the spectator an impression of infinite distance Kokoschka had entirely rejected central perspective, which, of course, he had never practised consistently, and had adopted a system of perspective employing two intersecting fields of vision. By this means he achieved a greater extension of the visual field. On this subject he wrote to the art-historian Hans M. Wingler: 'The fundamental difference between my conception and that of the Fauves seems to me to lie in the fact that Matisse and his circle came to prefer the two-dimensional surface, after having initially followed in the tracks of the Impressionists. But I could not think in any other way than spatially. Even after I had been wounded and my sense of touch disturbed, I could only arrive at the axial system characteristic of the new landscape paintings—which operates with the foci of a double ellipse and a conception of the world confined within space seen as spherical—by returning to earlier experiments regarding the sense of touch in space, which are embodied in the painting of Lyons.'

ARAB GIRLS 1928

Oil on canvas, $35 \times 51\frac{1}{8}$, HMW 234

Zürich, private collection

Kokoschka encountered the oriental world for the first time when he visited Africa.
At Tozeur he came across Bedouins, to which tribe the girls portrayed here belong.
The girls were afraid of having their portrait painted and had to be persuaded to
sit by a great deal of flattery and the gift of a lighter. Hence this sketch-like picture
was painted very quickly; and yet behind the passing moment that it captures we
can see all the excitement of the desert, the tension of nomads.

BUNCH OF AUTUMN FLOWERS 1928

Oil on canvas, $39\frac{3}{8} \times 31\frac{1}{2}$, HMW 238

Lugano, private collection

This picture was probably painted during a brief visit to Berlin. Indoor subjects are very rare among Kokoschka's works of this period. He was not interested in any theme which was merely a problem in composition. Hence this flame-like picture may be the expression of some particular experience. J. P. Hodin reports a conversation with Kokoschka in which the latter said of the basis of his pictures: 'There is a passage in the *Upanishads* which says that painted form is a spirit in the hierarchy of Maya, the world of phenomena, and therefore possesses form and a body. As long as I have been able to hold fast to a vision, I have lived on it. What else is there for me but to cling to the few roots I have within me? I have always been fascinated by inner processes. What is this fascination? Behind it lies a force. It is not a synthetic process. I can never learn anything; everything I have learnt, I have to forget again. I have never been able to copy myself, that would have been death. But when it holds fast to me, that is good. When it lets go of me, I am forsaken. I cannot believe in any life-surrogate. I could never bear to accomplish anything coldly.'

MARCEL VON NEMES 1929
Oil on canvas, $53\frac{1}{8} \times 37\frac{3}{8}$, HMW 245
Linz, Neue Galerie der Stadt Linz

Kokoschka met the eminent Hungarian collector in Munich on his way back from a trip to the Near East. Using earthy pigments, he portrays him as forceful and self-confident. By this time Kokoschka was already counted among the top flight of European painters. Max Liebermann wrote in the foreword to an exhibition catalogue: 'Of the artists now in the prime of life Kokoschka is unquestionably one of the most gifted . . . His most recent landscapes from Spain and England, which I have seen, prove that his storm and stress period is over. He has found himself, and as a result the path to timeless art lies open to him. Kokoschka is a born painter!'

VIENNA, SEEN FROM THE WILHELMINENBERG 1931

Oil on canvas, $36\frac{1}{4} \times 53\frac{1}{2}$, HMW 260

Vienna, Historisches Museum der Stadt

For one summer Kokoschka returned from his travels to his house in the Liebhartstal in Vienna. He was commissioned by the city council to paint a view of Vienna. The resulting picture shows the influence of Breughel's *Children's Games* in the Vienna Museum. Kokoschka made many studies relating to the composition of this painting, and a new allegorical trend makes its first appearance in it. Kokoschka himself wrote: 'It was my first picture showing a political outlook.' J. Meier-Graefe saw it soon after completion and wrote in an essay: 'With this most recent of his many pictures of towns Kokoschka has made things both easy and difficult for himself; easy, because he took at random the nearest landscape to his house; difficult, because he could hardly have picked a more thankless subject than this city over-rich in charms . . . The picture laughs, dances, sings. It would be almost impossible to personify the spirit of this city more accurately . . .'

SELF-PORTRAIT WITH CAP 1932

Oil on canvas, 38⅝×28, HMW 263

Epsom, private collection

This self-portrait was painted in Kokoschka's Paris studio during the serious economic crisis by which he himself was disastrously hard-hit. It is a proud assertion of his creative vocation. Kokoschka has painted few self-portraits and most of those during his early Viennese and Dresden periods. Some fourteen paintings are pure self-portraits and he has included himself in about eleven compositions containing several figures.

NOGENT-SUR-MARNE, VIADUCT 1932

Oil on canvas, 24×35⅞, HMW 264

New York, private collection

Kokoschka spent the year in which this picture was painted working almost uninterruptedly in his Paris studio. Again and again he was drawn by the organic interpenetration of nature and civilization in landscape. Once more the spreading surface of the water was an important element in the picture. The glazed colours portray the gaily charming atmosphere of the landscape round Paris in a manner that is almost like watercolour.

PRAGUE, CHARLES BRIDGE 1934

Oil on canvas, $34\frac{1}{4}\times48$, HMW 289

Prague, Nationalgalerie

From 1934 to 1938 Kokoschka lived in Prague, the city of his ancestors on his father's side. It is called the 'golden' or 'royal' city and of all the great cities of Europe it is the one most filled with spirits and mysteries. Here he painted fifteen large urban landscapes. This view across the Moldau to the Old Town shows Prague flooded with light, radiant and solemn like a mystic vision. The water, a barrier and a path at one and the same time, an element of distance, seems to lose all weight; as a medium for the transmission of light it is directly linked with the sky. These pictures of Prague have led to Kokoschka's being classified as an Impressionist; but the monumental pathos and the passionate, very personal vision expressed in them demand more of art, give it a different cause and a different goal than the Impressionist's programme. It is not that beautiful form is seen in the last analysis to be spiritual even in its most outward, most sensuous surface; on the contrary, it is the spirit that sees and shapes. The source of excitement in the picture is not the movement of matter and light; the seeing spirit finds in the agitation of the picture-surface the greatest possible outward and sensuous echo of its own perturbation.

POLPERRO II 1939

Oil on canvas, $23\frac{5}{8} \times 33\frac{1}{2}$, HMW 318

London, Tate Gallery

Kokoschka came to England with his wife in 1938, extremely poor and with
nothing but the bare essentials. After the outbreak of war they retired to Cornwall,
living in a small house on the cliffs near Polperro. To the depression due to the
terrible events of the day was added the anxiety of being an immigrant in a foreign
country at war. But his wife's courage and energy enabled Kokoschka to turn
even this time to advantage. Besides numerous aggressive political-allegorical
pictures he produced during the war years two Polperro landscapes and a few
portraits.

TOURBILLON DE SION 1947

Oil on canvas, $29\frac{1}{2} \times 41\frac{3}{8}$, HMW 341

Thalwil bei Zürich, private collection

Soon after the war Kokoschka made a trip to the Continent to check up on the situation and renew old contacts. Once again the mountains inspired a series of intense landscape paintings in strongly contrasting colours. In a large exhibition in Basle he found his paintings again after the crucial upheaval of the war, which had lain bare and destroyed so much. He stood in front of them alone 'to learn from them who he was and what had remained to him after all the tribulation. Kokoschka's painting blossomed again after years of suffering, during which he had stood firm and unafraid in his environment not only as an artist, but also as a man.' (J. P. Hodin)

LEUK AND THE RHÔNE VALLEY 1947

Oil on canvas, $29\frac{1}{2} \times 39\frac{3}{8}$, HMW 345

Vaduz, private collection

This is the last in the series of Swiss landscapes which Kokoschka painted in 1947. He was staying at Schloss Muzot as the guest of Werner Reinhart, the art-patron and friend of Rilke, whose portrait he also painted on this occasion. As he bade Switzerland a temporary farewell he painted this picture of Leuk looking down into the Rhône Valley in the hazy brightness of late summer. The same year, Theodor Heuss wrote in a review of the big Kokoschka exhibition: 'Many of these paintings we have seen before; how is it that they appear to us almost "classical"? No classicist could possibly give expression to such a temperament!'

SALZBURG 1950

Oil on canvas, $31\frac{1}{2}\times47\frac{1}{4}$, HMW 366

Munich, Bayerische Staatsgemäldesammlung

Kokoschka's largest figure composition to date, the triptych *The Prometheus Myth*, was painted in London. Kokoschka then went to stay in Salzburg at the invitation of Friedrich Welz; he considered settling permanently in his Austrian homeland. At all events, there were plans to establish in Salzburg, a city which appealed to Kokoschka because of its art-loving atmosphere, a summer course on the visual arts which would be a realization of his old idea of 'The School of Seeing'. Every summer since 1953 he has held a school in the Hohensalzburg Castle, which towers above the town in the background of this picture, not to train 'artists', but to teach young people to see through the experience of painting. From Salzburg Kokoschka went on to Bonn to fulfil a commission for the portrait of the President of the German Federal Republic, Theodor Heuss. Through the similarity of their humanist views the meeting between these two men deepened into friendship.

'GALATEA' 1953

Oil on canvas, $35\frac{7}{8} \times 28$, HMW 379

London, private collection

Shortly before Kokoschka settled finally in Switzerland he painted this portrait of an English noblewoman. The colours combine to create an atmosphere of exquisite light. This is a new vision of the human being portrayed with almost playful facility and yet with power and masterly skill. Kokoschka no longer stresses the extent to which man is at the mercy of his environment, as in his early works; in spite of his experiences of the destruction of so many values during the war, he emphasizes man's freedom and readiness to accept life.

PABLO CASALS 1954

Oil on canvas, $32\frac{1}{4} \times 25\frac{5}{8}$, HMW 383

New York, private collection

This portrait was painted while Kokoschka was working on the large triptych *Thermopylae*. Manuel Gasser wrote in an essay: 'The model has to be present from the first stroke of the brush to the last. Yet he need not "sit", he need not adopt a pose . . . He asked Pablo Casals to play finger exercises rather than proper music, because the divine notes of this 'cello distracted his attention from his work . . . What takes place between model and painter is a long, dogged, savage fight. The model poses, hides, disguises, refuses himself; the painter lies in wait, entices and teases the model and attacks in a flash when the other drops the mask for so much as a second. ("It was as though a lizard darted across his eyes," says Kokoschka, describing one of these moments of self-revelation.)'

LINZ 1955
Oil on canvas, $34\frac{5}{8} \times 45\frac{5}{8}$, HMW 387
Linz, Neue Galerie der Stadt Linz

In the foreground of this view of an industrial town stands nature. Kokoschka also gives expression to his tendency to see man and his world as a whole and to embed them in their natural environment in an essay on his *Thermopylae* triptych written at the same period: 'The task of the creative artist remains to give shape to his visual experience and, in a wider sense, to existence as a whole; for the dissolution, destruction, typification and atomization of personal life has already gone too far . . . What the proletarianized society of today needs most is retrospection . . .'

DELPHI 1956

Oil on canvas, $31\frac{7}{8} \times 44\frac{7}{8}$, HMW 393

Villeneuve, private collection

This view of the ruins at Delphi was painted on a journey through Greece in the spring of 1956. The monuments themselves do not play the leading role, but are absorbed into the vast, supra-historical, natural environment. Europe, too, is conceived by Kokoschka as a spiritual environment, as a heritage 'from the days of the Greeks'; it is more than merely a land rich in monuments to the past; it is for ever fruitful, for ever bringing forth fresh forms through contact with its origins. In an essay on the Prometheus myth he writes: 'Europe is not a geographical, but a cultural continent. If this concept is in danger of dissolving into nothingness, it means a loss to the whole of mankind. Throughout the world the younger generation is in the position of sons whose fathers have squandered an inheritance. But they themselves have not yet acquired the consciousness, which only comes with age, of also having obligations towards a future.' This concern with the transmission of tradition, as a duty to the future, is something Kokoschka tries to put into practice in his work.

RICHARD, MARGERY AND JOHN DAVIS 1958

Oil on canvas, $35\frac{3}{8} \times 47\frac{1}{4}$

Minneapolis, private collection

After the Second World War Kokoschka's work also became known in America; in 1949 he lectured as a guest professor at Boston University. In 1952 and 1953 he taught at the Minneapolis School of Art. In 1958 he painted the children of the director of the Boston Museum of Fine Arts. The children playing in the foreground, who seem almost to be floating among all the colours, acquire the value of a symbol of inexhaustible vitality; while the scintillating colours in the background combine to form a landscape.

VIEW OF THE THAMES 1959

Oil on canvas, $36\frac{2}{8} \times 48$

England, private collection

This view of the river from above Waterloo Bridge was painted during a visit by the artist to London in 1959 and it shows that his affection for the great sprawling city is undiminished. The high viewpoint occurs again and is particularly necessary in this case if both banks of the wide river are to be shown. Despite the sweeping horizon, there is no loss of intimacy. The congestion and weight of the city buildings concentrated in the left-hand quarter of the painting are balanced by the busy traffic on the water; both sides of the picture converge on the dome of St Paul's. The atmosphere of London comes through as perfectly as, in other pictures, the mood of Amsterdam, with its placid calm, Salzburg, with its feeling of intimacy, or Prague, with its fairy-tale, almost visionary, quality.

JOSHUA LOGAN 1960
Oil on canvas, $39\frac{1}{4} \times 32$
U.S.A., private collection

In this recent work Kokoschka's calligraphic brush-strokes seem to take on a new urgency; the treatment is probably freer than in any other portrait. Out of this whirlpool of fierce energy emerges an evocation of a man of huge dynamism—but a dynamism which can be controlled. Despite the vigour which is obviously the sitter's leading characteristic, he is shown here in thoughtful, relaxed mood. Joshua Logan, fifty-two years old when this portrait was painted, is one of America's most gifted men of the theatre; he has worked as director, writer and producer. Since the early years of the century when Kokoschka wrote plays such as *Mörder, Hoffnung der Frauen, Hiob* and *Der Brennende Dornbusch,* which exerted a profound influence on the German theatre of the day, he has maintained his interest in drama and other arts not directly connected with painting.

provisional catalogue of drawings by W. F. Arntz, 'Das graphische Werk Kokoschkas'. Prestel Verlag, Munich, 1950.

HANS MARIA WINGLER, *Künstler und Poeten. Bildniszeichnungen von Oskar Kokoschka.* Containing portrait sketches of Herwarth Walden, Else Laske-Schüler and other writers belonging to the literary group *Der Sturm.* Buchheim Verlag, Feldafing, 1954.

Oskar Kokoschka Lithographien. Introduction and interview by REMIGIUS NETZER. Verlag R. Piper and Co., Munich, 1956.

HANS MARIA WINGLER, *Oskar Kokoschka—Ein Lebensbild in Zeitgenössischen Dokumenten.* Verlag Albert Langen–Georg Müller, Munich, 1956.

HANS MARIA WINGLER, *Kokoschka—Fibel.* Verlag Galerie Welz, Salzburg, 1957.

Oskar Kokoschka. Catalogue of the exhibition in the Wiener Künstlerhaus, 19.5.1958–13.8.1958, ed. FRIEDRICH WELZ, pub. Österreichische Kulturvereinigung, Vienna, 1958.

The quotations in this book are all taken from the works listed above, except Kokoschka's definition of Expressionism which comes from his article 'Edvard Munchs Expressionismus' in the *Neue Züricher Zeitung,* Zürich, 18, 19, and 20 July, 1952.

LIST OF ILLUSTRATIONS

page	10	Pegasus 1951
	12	Snake Dance *c.* 1908
	13	*Illustration for* Mörder, Hoffnung der Frauen 1908
	14	*Title-page of* Die Träumenden Knaben 1908
	15	Woman Roller-Skating 1909
	17	Adolf Loos *c.* 1909
	18	Karl Kraus *c.* 1909
colour plate	19	Peter Baum 1910
	21	Self-portrait 1911
colour plate	22	Albert Ehrenstein 1914
	23	Karin Michaelis 1911
	24	*Sketch for* Lovers with Cat 1917
colour plate	25	Lovers with Cat 1917
	26	Nude at Table *c.* 1917
	27	Reclining Child 1917
	27	*Two illustrations for Dirszthay's* Lob des Hoben Verstandes 1917
	28, 29, 31	*Studies for* Woman in Blue 1919
	30	Seated Woman *c.* 1920
	32	The Artist and the Muse 1921
	32	*Illustration for Dirszthay's* Der Unentrinnbare 1923
	33	Maria Orska 1922
colour plate	34	Dresden, Bridge over the Elbe 1923
colour plate	35	Girl with Flowers in her Hair *c.* 1930
colour plate	36	Genoa, View of Harbour 1932–3
colour plate	37	The Visit 1934
	38	La Passionaria 1937
colour plate	40	Cathleen, Countess of Drogheda 1943–6
	41	Poster *c.* 1945

Colour plates page 45

45	Still-life with Pineapple 1907
47	Old Man. Father Hirsch 1907
49	Children Playing 1909
51	Still-life with Sheep and Hyacinth 1909
53	Cat (sketch) 1910
55	Hugo Caro 1910
57	Flight into Egypt 1911
59	Tre Croci, Dolomites 1913
61	The Bride of the Wind 1914
63	Lady with Parrot 1916
65	Self-portrait 1917
67	The Friends 1917–18
69	Woman in Blue 1919
71	Dresden, New Town II 1921
73	Boats near the Dogana, Venice 1924
75	Madrid, Puerta del Sol 1925
77	Kloveniersburgval, Amsterdam 1925
79	London, Large Thames Landscape I 1926
81	Tiger-lion 1926
83	Richmond Terrace 1926
85	Chamonix and Mont Blanc 1927
87	Lac d'Annecy I 1927
89	Lyons 1927
91	Arab Girls 1928
93	Bunch of Autumn Flowers 1928
95	Marcel von Nemes 1929
97	Vienna, seen from the Wilhelminenburg 1931
99	Self-portrait with Cap 1932
101	Nogent-sur-Marne, Viaduct 1932
103	Prague, Charles Bridge 1934
105	Polperro II 1939
107	Tourbillon de Sion 1947
109	Leuk and the Rhône Valley 1947
111	Salzburg 1950
113	Hamburg, View of the Harbour 1951
115	'Galatea' 1953
117	Pablo Casals 1954
119	Linz 1955
121	Delphi 1956
123	Richard, Margery and John Davis 1958
125	View of the Thames 1959
127	Joshua Logan 1960